Courage and Quick Thinking

A TRUE ADVENTURE READER

Lisa Yount

 **J. Weston Walch, Publisher**
Portland, Maine

Cover photograph taken by Richard V. Procopio

1   2   3   4   5   6   7   8   9   10

ISBN 0-8251-2215-5

To the memory of my father,
Stanley G. Yount

Life with him was always
an adventure!

Contents

Introduction

Just about everyone loves an adventure story. Why? Maybe it's because a secret adventurer lives inside all of us. Adventure doesn't come often to most people's lives—and perhaps that's just as well. But as we watch or read about someone climbing a mountain or saving a child from a burning building, we wish just a little that we could be up there showing what we could really do if we only had the chance.

Living through an adventure sometimes depends on bodily strength or endurance. But even more, it depends on the mind and heart. It depends on who the adventurer is inside. Adventurers must be able to think quickly. They must be willing to try unexpected solutions to problems. And they must have the power to put fear aside and give everything they have to doing the job they need to do. Adventurers risk their safety, even their lives. They are willing to bet that much on themselves.

In this book you will find twelve short stories of adventure. The stories happened in different times and places. But the adventurer in every one of them is a real person. (One story comes from a legend, or long-told folk tale. There is reason to think, though, that even this story may be based on fact.)

You will meet many kinds of adventurers in these stories. They are men, women, even children. They come from many races and cultures. Some, the scientists and explorers, go looking for adventure. Others are ordinary people who discover that adventure has found them. But however their adventure starts, all of them face the challenge that the adventure offers them, and win.

As you read these stories, I hope you will let the adventurer inside you come out. Pretend that the challenge in each adventure has been offered to you, and think about how you would meet it. To help you do this, each story is divided into two parts. The first part stops at the moment when the challenge is greatest. At the end of this part is an activity that asks you to try to solve the adventurer's problem. The second part of the story tells how the adventurer solved it. After that part is another activity that lets you use what you have learned in the story to make an adventure of your own.

Happy adventuring!

Rescued by Two Chickens

"**W**anted: Harriet Tubman**, also called Harriet Greene. Middle-aged Negro woman, very dark skin. About five feet tall. Escaped slave, wanted for stealing other slaves. $40,000 reward."

"My goodness, what a lot of money!" cried the woman in the train. She had just read the poster aloud to her friends. "I've never seen such a high reward for an escaped slave. The slave owners must want this Tubman woman very badly."

A few rows behind her, a small African-American woman huddled low in her seat. Her big, floppy bonnet hid the smile on her face. "Thank you for reading that poster to me," she thought. She herself did not know how to read. Until the other woman spoke, she had not known what the poster said. She did know the face drawn on it, though. It was her own.

Harriet Tubman knew very well why the slave owners of the South wanted her so much. She had already rescued about three hundred people from them. Those people had been slaves like herself. To the slave owners, they were property, like a horse or a wagon. To Tubman, they were her people.

The slaves of the South called Tubman "Moses." They knew that, like Moses in the Bible, she led her people to freedom.

In those years just before the Civil War, many people helped slaves to escape. Some of those helpers, like Tubman, were black. Others were white. The slaves were led from one safe house to another. Their path was sometimes called the "Underground Railroad." Always they went north, where slavery was against the law. Time after time, Tubman went south to start a new group of slaves on their journey. She risked her life every time.

Just before she got on this train, in fact, Tubman had left a group of slaves with friends. The friends would help the slaves go farther north. Tubman herself was traveling north on the train.

Hearing about the poster, however, changed Tubman's plans. She knew that north was the direction the slaveholders would expect her to go. People trying to get the reward would look closely at any African-American woman traveling north.

But what about an African-American woman traveling south? Tubman chuckled. No one, surely, would guess that she might go back to the very place where she was in such danger. Strange as it might seem, then, going south would be the safest thing for her to do.

Tubman got off the train at the next station. She boarded another train going south. Then she left that train at the most unlikely place of all. It was a little village. Tubman had worked there when she was a slave. The master for whom she had worked still lived there.

But Tubman had a plan to keep herself from being recognized. She pulled her bonnet low over her face. She walked bent over like an old, old woman. And she bought two live chickens at the village market. She carried the chickens with her. Their legs were tied together with a string.

Tubman's plan was soon put to the test. She turned a corner and gasped. Her old master was coming toward her!

Before you read on . . .

> Why do you think Tubman bought the chickens? How might they help her keep her master from spotting her?

Harriet Tubman's old master was still some way down the village street. He had not seen her. Good, Tubman thought. If her plan worked, he would see her, all right. But he wouldn't collect any $40,000 reward!

Tubman's two chickens hung from the string over her arm. Each end of the string was tied around one chicken's legs. Now, without letting anyone see what she was doing, she untied the string.

All at once the street was full of noise and feathers. The chickens, suddenly free, squawked loudly. They flapped their wings as they fluttered to the ground. Confused, they ran around in circles. Their running stirred up clouds of dust.

Tubman stooped over to grab at the "escaped" chickens. The dust they raised hid her almost completely. Everyone on the street stopped to watch the fuss. But no one really looked at the woman who was the center of it.

Tubman went on chasing the chickens until her master had walked by. "Silly old woman!" she heard him laugh as he passed.

Tubman smiled. "The joke is on you," she thought. How the man would have cursed if he had known that he had almost stepped on the escaped slave he wanted so badly!

When her master was gone, Tubman stood up. She watched the chickens flap excitedly down the street. "I hope you stay free, just like my people," she said softly.

Make Your Own Adventure

> Suppose you have to pass through a group of people who know you, but you don't want them to recognize you. How could you disguise yourself? What changes would you make in the way you look? What changes would you make in the way you act? Write a description, or draw and label a picture or pictures showing your disguise and how you would use it.

Adventuring in Real Life

Follow your teacher's directions for these activities.

—— Reliving the Adventure ——

1. How did Tubman learn that slaveholders were offering a high reward for her?

   _____

   _____

2. Why did the slave owners offer such a high reward?

   _____

   _____

3. Why did the slaves call Tubman "Moses"?

   _____

   _____

4. How did slaves escape from the South?

_____

_____

5. What did Tubman do after she learned about the reward? Why did she do it?

_____

_____

6. Why was getting off at the village dangerous for Tubman?

_____

_____

7. How did Tubman disguise herself?

_____

_____

8. How did Tubman use the two chickens she had bought?

_____

_____

—— Thinking About It ——

1. Why might some white people have wanted to help black slaves escape?

2. The escaped chickens made everyone look at Tubman. How did they also keep her master from recognizing her?

—— Exploring Further ——

1. Find out more about Harriet Tubman. What other adventures did she have when she helped slaves escape? Find out more about the Underground Railroad, too. Who were some of the people who helped in it? How did they help slaves escape?

2. With a group of your classmates, act out a story about Harriet Tubman or the Underground Railroad. You might act out the story you just read. Or you might act out another one that you find in your reading. You might want to show your skit to parents or to students from another class.

3. Find out more about the Civil War. Slavery was one reason the war was fought. What were some other reasons? What states fought on the North or Union side? What states fought on the South or Confederate side? What were some of the major battles of the war? How was the war finally won? Write down what you find out.

Adventuring on Paper

—— Exploring Words ——

The slaves thought Harriet Tubman was like Moses in the Bible because she led her people to freedom. They gave her the nick-name "Moses."

Write the names of five famous people below. They can be people living today, or they can be people from history or legend. After each name, write down the sort of person who might be given that name as a nickname.

Example:
Famous person: John Henry (black man of legend who was supposed to be very strong)
Person who might be given nickname: someone very strong

1. Famous person: _____

   Person who might be given nickname: _____

   _____

2. Famous person: _____

   Person who might be given nickname: _____

   _____

3. Famous person: _____

   Person who might be given nickname: _____

   _____

4. Famous person: _____

   Person who might be given nickname: _____

   _____

5. Famous person: _____

   Person who might be given nickname: _____

   _____

—— Exploring Sentences ——

Pronouns are words that stand for nouns. Rewrite each sentence below, using pronouns to substitute for the underlined nouns.

1. Harriet Tubman saw a poster that offered a reward for <u>Harriet Tubman</u>.

   _____

2. The slave owners wanted Tubman because <u>the slave owners</u> thought <u>Tubman</u> had stolen <u>the slave owners'</u> property.

   _____

3. When slaves wanted to escape, both black and white people helped <u>the slaves</u>.

   _____

4. Tubman got on a train going south and then left <u>the train</u> at a small village.

   _____

5. Tubman's old master passed right by <u>Tubman</u>, but <u>the master</u> did not recognize <u>Tubman</u>.

   _____

6. When Tubman let her chickens go, <u>the chickens</u> made a fuss that saved <u>Tubman's</u> life.

   _____

—— Exploring Writing ——

Some slaves wrote (or told their stories to other people who wrote) about their lives during slavery. If you can, find and read some of these slave stories. Your library may have some.

Imagine what it would be like to be a slave. What would you hate most about it? How would you and your friends keep your spirits up? What plans for escape would you make?

Pretend you are a slave writing your story before the Civil War. Or, if you would rather, imagine that you are a slave in some future society. Write a few paragraphs telling what your life as a slave is like.

Ghosts of the Gobi

Finding his way across the Gobi Desert was not really so hard, Hsuan-tsang thought. He only had to follow the path that other travelers had taken. The path was marked by things that the travelers had left behind.

Piles of bones, for instance. Some of the bones no doubt were from meat that the travelers had eaten. Others may have belonged to the travelers themselves. The desert was not kind to those who made poor choices or had bad luck. Neither were the robbers who often attacked them.

Hsuan-tsang had vowed that none of these dangers would stop him. He was a monk. He had given his life to religion. Buddhism, the religion he followed, had begun in far-off India. Hsuan-tsang had questions that he felt only the holy men and books of India could answer. He had decided, therefore, to travel from China to India. He did not care how hard the trip would be.

Hsuan-tsang wished he could have gone with a caravan, like earlier travelers. It was much safer to cross the desert with a large group of people. But in these early years of the seventh century, no caravans were leaving China. The emperor had ordered that no one was to go out of the country. Hsuan-tsang had had to leave the capital city alone and in secret.

The monk's only friend on his long journey was his horse. The man who had sold it to him swore that the animal had been across the Gobi fifteen times. If Hsuan-tsang could not find his way, perhaps the horse could.

Hsuan-tsang and his horse had been plodding through the sandy wasteland for days now. During all that time they had seen no other living thing. The monk was all the more amazed, then, to see hundreds of men suddenly riding toward him.

The monk stared at the riders. They seemed to be everywhere on the sandy plain. Some were on horses. Others rode camels. Sunlight glittered on their flags and long, pointed lances. Hsuan-tsang thought he could hear drums and shouting voices. As the first of the riders came near, he could even see the fur and felt on their clothing.

Who were these men? Were they soldiers? Were they robbers? How had they appeared out of nowhere? A thousand questions swam through Hsuan-tsang's mind. But these questions were all replaced by a bigger one as the riders thundered by.

As soon as the riders passed him, they vanished!

Before you read on . . .

> Who or what do you think the riders were?

More and more of the strange desert riders swirled past Hsuan-tsang. As some came close, they changed into fantastic shapes. They looked more like demons than men. Others rode up to him and disappeared.

The sight would have been enough to frighten anyone. Yet the Chinese monk seemed to hear voices that calmed him. "Do not fear! Do not fear!" they said.

Hsuan-tsang did not know what the riders were. It was clear that they were not real. Perhaps they were evil spirits of the desert. Perhaps they were made out of nothing by his lonely mind. Whatever they were, he was no longer afraid of them. He pushed on.

Many miles later, Hsuan-tsang came to a danger that he took much more seriously. It was the first of the watchtowers on the Chinese border. He could see lookouts pacing along its top. It would be better, he thought, if they did not see him.

The monk and his horse hid behind a sand dune until night fell. Then Hsuan-tsang crept out quietly. He had seen an oasis, one of the desert's rare water holes, west of the tower. He was very thirsty. In the dark, perhaps, he could reach the water safely.

At first luck seemed to be with Hsuan-tsang. He and his horse reached the water hole. He drank and washed his hands. Then he bent over to fill his water jug.

That was when Hsuan-tsang's luck ran out. He cried out in pain as a flying arrow scraped his knee. Before he could turn around, another arrow whizzed past.

The lookouts must have spotted him. "I am a priest from the capital! Do not shoot me!" he shouted into the darkness.

"Come forward and show yourself!" a voice demanded.

Hsuan-tsang had no choice but to obey. He led his horse toward the watchtower. Guards opened the gate and came out. Holding torches above his head, they studied him carefully.

The guards recognized the monk's robe that Hsuan-tsang wore. "Well, you are indeed a priest," one said. "Come and speak to our commander, Wang-siang."

Hsuan-tsang was soon seated by the commander, next to a roaring fire. "I know all the priests in this province of Ho-si," Wang-siang said. "You certainly are not one of them. So perhaps your story is true. Tell me, why are you traveling against the emperor's orders?"

Hsuan-tsang explained that he was going to India to seek religious knowledge.

"Well, I suppose there is no harm in that. We will let you go. What you seek must mean a lot to you if you are willing to cross this desert alone for it."

Hsuan-tsang nodded. The commander did not know the half of it, he thought. He wondered what Wang-siang would say if he told him that he had already had to face an army of ghosts!

Make Your Own Adventure

Explain how you would draw a picture of Hsuan-tsang and the ghostly riders. How would you make your picture suggest that the riders were not real?

Adventuring in Real Life

Follow your teacher's directions for these activities.

—— Reliving the Adventure ——

1. How did Hsuan-tsang find his way across the Gobi Desert?

   _____

   _____

2. Why did Hsuan-tsang want to cross the Gobi?

   _____

   _____

3. Why did he have to travel alone and in secret?

   _____

   _____

4. What frightening sight did Hsuan-tsang see as he crossed the desert?

   _____

   _____

5. What helped Hsuan-tsang guess that the figures he saw were not real?

   _____

   _____

6. Why did the soldiers in the watchtower shoot at Hsuan-tsang?

   _____

   _____

7. Why did the commander let Hsuan-tsang go?

   _____

   _____

—— Thinking About It ——

1. Why was Hsuan-tsang more worried about the soldiers in the watchtowers than about the riders?

2. What part of Hsuan-tsang's experience did he probably imagine?

—— Exploring Further ——

1. A later traveler called Marco Polo also wrote about the ghosts of the Gobi. (The riders were probably a mirage.) Marco Polo was an Italian. He visited China in the late thirteenth century. Later he wrote about his trip. Find out more about Marco Polo's journey. What adventures did he have? What did he see in China?

2. Look at a map of Asia. Draw a line from China to India. If Hsuan-tsang made his journey by land today, what countries would he pass through?

3. What are some good safety rules for walking or driving in the desert today? You may be able to find some in library books. Ask someone who knows about outdoor survival to tell you others. Make a class list of rules for traveling in the desert.

4. Find out more about ancient China. The Chinese invented many things long ago. Find out how they made paper. Find out how they used rockets. Find out about the Great Wall they built. When was it built? Who built it and why? Tell your classmates what you learn.

Adventuring on Paper

—— Exploring Words ——

Each word below comes from the story about Hsuan-tsang. For each word, write a word or phrase that appears near it that can help you guess the word's meaning.

Example: demon (word)
  fantastic shapes (phrase)

1. monk

———————————————————————

2. caravan

———————————————————————

3. lances

———————————————————————

4. oasis

———————————————————————

—— Exploring Sentences ——

Write five sentences that could be part of a desert adventure. In each sentence, use a word that you think other people might not know. (You can use some of the words from the **Exploring Words** exercise if you want to.) Put at least one word clue in your sentence that can help people guess the meaning of your unusual word.

1. _____
   _____

2. _____
   _____

3. _____
   _____

4. _____
   _____

5. _____
   _____

—— Exploring Writing ——

What questions are so important to you that you would go a long way to have them answered? Where might you go to find answers to those questions? Write a paragraph or two about your journey. Tell what you think you would find out.

Face to Face with a Leopard

Mary Kingsley couldn't stand it a minute longer. She would have to do something about that leopard.

The big cat had been snarling and roaring all night. Kingsley could hardly help hearing it. The trap that held it was only a few yards from the hut she was trying to sleep in. To the Africans who lived in this village, she knew, the leopard's cries were the sounds of a defeated enemy. To her, though, they simply meant an animal in pain.

Anger and determination kept Kingsley from being afraid. She hurried outside. She didn't even wait to put on her boots.

Kingsley had almost reached the leopard trap before she noticed her bare feet. When she did become aware of them, they brought her more terror than the leopard did. She knew that poisonous snakes hunted along the ground. In the dark, she was likely to step on one. African villagers stayed in their huts at night because of this danger.

Well, what was done was done, Kingsley thought. She ran just as much risk going back to her hut as going on. At least the fear of snakes would keep anyone from trying to stop her in what she was about to do.

The leopard was just ahead. Its eyes blazed like lanterns. As Kingsley came closer, it roared and bared its teeth. It pulled uselessly against the rope that held it.

Wooden stakes had been driven into the ground all around the animal. They made a kind of cage. Kingsley knew that the villagers planned to leave the leopard there. In time, it would wear itself out. Finally it would die.

But not if Mary Kingsley had anything to say about the matter! Kingsley stepped forward. She pulled out the first of the stakes. Then she followed with the others, one by one.

The leopard, of course, did not understand that it was being rescued. It lunged out at Kingsley in rage. She barely stayed clear of its raking claws. At one point, in fact, a claw ripped her long, dark skirt from waist to ankle.

Even then, Kingsley did not stop. Finally all the stakes were out except the last one. This held the end of the rope that had trapped the leopard. Kingsley could not reach it without getting too close to the angry animal. She was sure, though, that the leopard could pull that stake up by itself. Then, no doubt, it would run away into the forest.

Kingsley found that she was partly right. The leopard indeed had no trouble pulling the last stake. It did not run away, however. Instead it began to walk around her, circling closer and closer.

Before you read on . . .

Make a list of at least three things that Mary Kingsley could have done at this moment. Then draw a line under the one you think she decided to do. At the bottom of your paper, write a sentence or two telling why you think she would have made that choice.

The leopard sniffed Mary Kingsley's skirt. It snarled softly.

Kingsley was not sure whether she could have moved if she had wanted to. Fear seemed to have pinned her feet to the ground. She felt trapped as surely as the leopard had been.

She also knew better than to run away. If she had done so, the leopard would have thought she was its prey. It would have attacked her at once.

Mary Kingsley had found before that a strange thing happened to her when she became frightened enough. She got cross. That was what seemed to take place now. She spoke to the leopard like an angry schoolteacher. "Go home, you fool!" she commanded.

Whatever the leopard had expected Kingsley to do, it wasn't this. The startled cat stared at her. Then it turned around. It padded away quietly into the forest.

This was neither the first nor the last time that an unexpected act saved Mary Kingsley's life. Of course, her being in Africa at all was unexpected. At that time, the 1890's, most English women never left their own country. They certainly did not go to Africa. The few that did were usually either colonial officials' wives or missionaries. They stayed with their husbands or fellow workers. They did not travel through the rain forest, as Kingsley did, alone except for native guides.

But Kingsley loved the unexpected. She loved Africa, too. Her father, a world traveler, had given her an interest in other cultures. She also wanted to know about the plants and animals in faraway places. While she was in Africa, she collected fish for the British Museum. She also took notes about African culture, religion, and law. Later she wrote books and gave talks about Africa. Her work helped Europeans learn to understand and respect Africans in a way that few had done before.

Make Your Own Adventure

Suppose you are visiting a people whose way of life is very different from yours. You do not speak each other's languages. How would you try to show the people that you want to be friends? How would you ask for things you need? How could you learn about the people's way of life? Write a few sentences telling about your ideas.

Adventuring in Real Life

Follow your teacher's directions for these activities.

—— Reliving the Adventure ——

1. What was keeping Mary Kingsley awake?

_____

_____

2. Why was Kingsley frightened when she noticed that she had forgotten to put on her boots?

_____

_____

3. How did Kingsley go about freeing the leopard?

_____

_____

4. What did the leopard do once it was free?

_____

_____

5. What did Kingsley do to drive the leopard away?

_____

_____

6. Why was Kingsley's trip to Africa unusual?

_____

_____

7. Why did she want to come to Africa?

_____

_____

8. What did Kingsley do after her trip?

_____

_____

—— **Thinking About It** ——

1. Why did Mary Kingsley want to free the leopard?

2. Why do you think the villagers trapped the leopard?

—— **Exploring Further** ——

1. Mary Kingsley was one of a number of British explorers who visited Africa in the late nineteenth century. Some others were Richard Burton, David Livingstone, James Bruce, and Samuel and Florence Baker. Find out about one of these or some other nineteenth-century European explorer of Africa. Why did that explorer come to Africa? What did he or she learn there? What adventures did the explorer have? Tell your classmates what you find out.

2. At the time Mary Kingsley went to Africa, most of Africa was controlled by European countries. Those countries had divided Africa into different colonies. Today, most African countries are independent. Many of them changed their names when they became free. Make a chart with these headings:

Name today	Name as a colony	European country that controlled colony	Year of Independence

Fill in the chart with as many African countries as you can. Use an almanac or an encyclopedia to help you.

3. Have an Africa Day in your classroom. Divide your class into groups. Have one group learn about African music. Have one learn about African religions. Have one learn about African clothes. Have one learn about African art. Have one learn about African foods. Other groups might want to learn other things about traditional African ways of life. (Africa has many different peoples. Each people has its own traditions.

Thus, for example, there are many different kinds of African music or art.) On Africa Day, share what the groups have learned. Bring in things to show if you can. For example, the food group might bring in an African dish they have cooked. The music group might play records of African music.

Adventuring on Paper

—— Exploring Words ——

Words that sound like other words but are spelled differently and have different meanings are called **homonyms**. Below are some words from the story about Mary Kingsley. Next to each word, write a homonym for that word. The first one is done for you.

1. to _____two_____   4. stake _____

2. knew _____   5. prey _____

3. bare _____   6. know _____

—— Exploring Sentences ——

The words below are from the Mary Kingsley story. Each can have more than one meaning. Write two sentences for each word. Use one of the word's meanings in one sentence. Use another meaning in the other sentence.

1. stand _____

_____

2. yards _____

_____

3. driven _____

_____

4. clear _____

_____

5. cross _____

_____

6. padded _____

_____

—— Exploring Writing ——

Suppose that a person from a distant land comes to your town or your part of the city. You might even want to imagine that this person is from Mars. The visitor has never been to the United States before. He or she knows nothing at all about American life.

Now imagine that you are the person from Mars. What things and actions do you see that seem most strange to you? What guesses do you make about what these things mean? What do you learn about the people you are visiting? What do you like or dislike about them? Write a paragraph or two telling about your visit to this strange land.

Dive to Save a Life

At first Kondiba Gaikwad couldn't tell what was going on. He heard people running and shouting in the street outside. What they were saying, however, was not clear.

Then a woman's shrill cry split the air. Her words were plain. "Someone's fallen in the well!"

Gaikwad knew about the well. Yelenbai Jambure, his landlady, had described it to him. It was just a big, funnel-shaped hole in the ground. No wall surrounded it. No top covered it when it was not being used. People getting water from it had to stand or sit on a slippery tree trunk laid across it.

The well water itself was an ugly greenish black, Mrs. Jambure said. It was not very clean. But it was just about the only water that the people of Golibar had. Golibar was a slum in the large city of Bombay, India. The people of Golibar had very little of anything.

Kondiba Gaikwad could not see the well for himself. He had been blind since he was eight years old. A terrible sickness called smallpox had destroyed his sight. At that time he had lived in a village several hundred miles from Bombay.

Gaikwad still missed his home. But the village had run out of food during a famine several years before. Everyone who could had left. Gaikwad had come to Bombay. At first he had tried to earn money by selling brooms. Few people had bought them, however. Now, in 1975, the 25-year-old man lived by begging. He hated it, but there seemed to be nothing else to do.

He could do something now, though. "Quick, lead me to the well," Gaikwad told Mrs. Jambure.

"Why? How will that help?"

"You will see. Just take me there."

Mrs. Jambure led Gaikwad to the well. Crying people stood around it. Most were women and children. The men of Golibar were away at work.

"Who has fallen in?" Mrs. Jambure asked one of the women.

"It's Arvind—Arvind Pimpalkar. He fell off the tree trunk when he was pulling up a bucket of water."

Mrs. Jambure and Gaikwad knew Arvind. He was only fourteen. Like many of the people in Golibar, he could not swim.

Two boys about Arvind's age were already in the well. They had tried to rescue Arvind, the woman said. Arvind, however, had sunk down into the well. The other boys could only paddle a little. They did not know how to dive down to search for him.

Gaikwad did not listen any longer. He pulled off most of his clothes. Then he jumped into the slimy water of the well.

Before you read on . . .

How could Kondiba Gaikwad rescue Arvind? Write down three things he might do.

As a boy, Kondiba Gaikwad had been a fine swimmer. He could dive well, too. In the village, he and his friends had had a game. They would throw shiny pieces of broken pots into a well. Then they would take turns diving down to pick them up. Young Kondiba had been able to dive deepest of all.

But that had been many years ago. Gaikwad had done no swimming or diving since then. During most of those years he had had very little to eat. Lack of good food had made him weak. Could he still hold his breath long enough to dive to the bottom of a deep well?

He knew he would soon find out. Floating in the water, Gaikwad took several deep breaths. Then he dived. Seconds later, he touched the rocks at the bottom of the well. Frantically he felt through the mud and slimy weeds. He found nothing.

Gasping, Gaikwad came to the surface. The women around the well wailed louder when they saw him. Arvind Pimpalkar had been under water for two minutes now. If Gaikwad did not find him quickly, the boy would drown.

Gaikwad dived again. This time he tried to search the well bottom in a more organized way. He was able to stay down longer this time. But it didn't matter. He still could not find Arvind.

Gaikwad was very tired now. Still, he felt he had to try once more. He surfaced, then dived a third time.

This time Gaikwad's searching fingers touched something that wasn't a water weed. It was cloth! He followed it down and felt a leg. It must be Arvind, tangled in the weeds.

Gaikwad couldn't hold his breath much longer. But if he went to the surface again, he would waste precious seconds. Worse still, he might not be able to find Arvind when he returned. He had to bring the boy up this time—somehow.

Gaikwad needed a good way to hang onto the boy. Arvind's wet skin was slippery. His clothing was likely to tear. Gaikwad felt along Arvind's body until he found the boy's belt. He got a firm grip on the belt. Then he yanked. He had to pull several times to get Arvind free of the weeds.

Now Gaikwad tried to head for the surface. But he was just about worn out. Arvind weighed almost as much as he did. He felt as if he were trying to swim with a huge stone tied to his arm. If he did not let go of Arvind, he himself seemed sure to drown.

The twenty-foot well seemed as deep as an ocean. Somehow, though, Kondiba Gaikwad made it to the top. He was still holding Arvind's belt.

Other people reached down to pull Arvind out of the well. Some began to give the boy artificial respiration. After a minute or two, Arvind began to breathe on his own.

Gaikwad was almost too tired to care. All he could think about was catching his own breath. He hung onto the side of the well until he began to breathe normally again. Then he climbed out. People helped him up and hugged him. Yelenbai Jambure led him home. There, exhausted, Kondiba Gaikwad fell asleep.

Arvind was taken to the hospital. He came back the next day. He went at once to Gaikwad. He bowed and touched the blind man's feet in thanks.

Arvind was not the only one who was grateful. Newspapers picked up the story of the boy's rescue. High officials praised Gaikwad. Better still, people sent him money as a reward for his courage.

Gaikwad used the money to move out of Bombay. He went back to a town near his old village. He started a small business there. With luck, he thought, he would never have to beg again.

Make Your Own Adventure

Get a box with a lid. Cut a hole in the lid just big enough for a hand to go through. Then put several familiar things in the box. Put in one or two unusual things, too. Don't put in anything sharp or dangerous.

Now trade boxes with a partner. Put your hand inside your partner's box. Feel each thing in the box. Then write down what you think is in the box.

Check each other's lists. How many things in your partner's box were you able to identify by touch? How many things in your box could your partner identify?

Adventuring in Real Life
Follow your teacher's directions for these activities.

—— Reliving the Adventure ——

1. In what ways was the well in Golibar dangerous? Why wasn't it fixed?

_____

_____

2. Who fell in the well? Why did he fall?

_____

_____

3. Why did Kondiba Gaikwad have to beg for a living?

_____

_____

4. Who tried to rescue Arvind before Gaikwad? Why didn't they succeed?

_____

_____

5. Why did Gaikwad think he might be able to rescue Arvind? What besides his blindness might keep him from succeeding?

_____

_____

6. How did Gaikwad finally find Arvind?

_____

_____

7. How did Gaikwad bring Arvind to the surface?

_____

_____

8. How did rescuing Arvind change Gaikwad's life?

_____

_____

—— Thinking About It ——

1. How might the people of Golibar fix the well to make it safer?

2. If someone begged for money from you, would you give the person some? Why or why not? If your answer is "some-times" or "maybe," what helps you decide?

—— Exploring Further ——

1. Find out about life in India today. What are some of the ways that people there earn a living? How is the government trying to help poor people? What problems remain?

2. If you can, ask a speaker from a group that helps disabled people to come to class. Think of questions to ask the speaker. For example, how can disabled people be helped to get jobs? What laws or programs concerning disabled people would the group like to see passed? How does the group recommend that others treat disabled people?

3. No one today could go blind for the reason that Kondiba Gaikwad did. Find out why. Ask a librarian to help you learn about smallpox. Find out how this terrible disease was finally removed from the earth.

4. What rules should people follow to be safe in the water? If someone is in danger of drowning, how can he or she be helped? You might ask someone from a group like the American Red Cross these questions. Or you might learn the answers from a book about first aid. Tell your classmates what you find out.

Adventuring on Paper

—— Exploring Words ——

The same sound can be spelled differently in different words. In each pair of words below, circle the letters that make the sound that is the same in both words. The first one is done for you.

1. h(ear)d   b(ir)d   4. clean   seen
2. plain   cane   5. slum   come
3. cry   die   6. blind   mined

—— Exploring Sentences ——

Words rhyme when they end in the same sound. For example, the two words in each word pair in the last exercise rhyme. For each sentence below, write another sentence. The last word in the second sentence should rhyme with the last word in the first sentence. Try to have your two-sentence rhyme make sense.

Example:

The well was a danger for people getting *water.*

"Try to be careful!" the mother warned her *daughter.*

1. Gaikwad was blind, but he was brave.

   _____

2. Gaikwad hated a beggar's life.

   _____

3. Gaikwad dived into the well.

   _____

4. Arvind was trapped among the weeds.

_____

5. Gaikwad brought Arvind onto the land.

_____

6. The newspapers printed Gaikwad's story.

_____

—— Exploring Writing ——

Think of a time when you made yourself do something even though you were so tired that you did not think you possibly could. If you can't remember a time like that, imagine one. Then write about it. Why did you want to do the thing in spite of being tired? How did you make yourself go on when you wanted to stop? How did you feel afterward?

Moremi Saves Ife

Long ago, the Yoruba say, Ife was the richest city of their people. (The Yoruba live in what is southern Nigeria today. Nigeria is a country in West Africa.) Ife, the Yoruba say, had fields of grain all around it. Its markets were full of fruit and yams.

Yet the rich city seemed doomed to become a poor city. Every time Ife's crops were gathered, fearsome beings came out of the rain forest. They wore clothing of straw. Horrible masks covered their faces. They looked like *egunguns*, evil spirits from the Land of the Dead.

Making a terrifying noise, the evil spirits dashed into Ife. The people of the city were badly frightened. They hid in the forest. While the people were gone, the spirits stole all the city's food. Then they disappeared as quickly as they had come.

This happened not once but many times. The people of Ife grew hungry and sad. Even their Oba, or king, was in despair. "Why should we bother to plant and harvest our crops? Why should we bother to do anything?" he cried one morning. "Whatever we make or grow, the evil spirits take away."

"A woman named Moremi is here to see you," the king's chief counselor announced just then.

"A woman? How odd! Well, send her in," said the king.

"I think I can help you fight the evil spirits," Moremi told Ife's ruler. "I want to learn more about them. Maybe they are not spirits at all. Why should spirits want to steal our food? Next time they come, I will hide in the city and watch them."

"You can't do that!" the king protested. "Not even our bravest warrior is willing to stay in Ife when the spirits come. Besides, women are not allowed to look at spirit beings. You will only be killed if you try."

"I don't care what you say," Moremi said. "I will do it."

The king called the wise men of Ife together. He told them about Moremi's plan. Then he asked what he should do.

"Let her try it," the wisest man said at last. "Maybe she will be killed. Maybe she won't. But if somebody doesn't do something soon, we will all die."

So Moremi waited until the egunguns came again to Ife. Everyone else ran away. Moremi, however, stayed behind in her hut. The spirits found her there. They tied her with ropes. They dragged her into the forest along with all of Ife's food.

Once they were deep in the forest, the "spirits" took off their masks. Moremi saw that she had been right. The thieves were human beings.

Now the robbers began to talk and laugh. Listening carefully, Moremi soon learned all about them. They were men from a faraway city named Ile-Igbo. Crops did not grow well in Ile-Igbo. Its people were hungry. Then one day a hunter from Ile-Igbo had become lost in the forest. He had wandered so far that he had found Ife. He had seen how much food the city had.

In time the hunter had found his way back to Ile-Igbo. He had told the city's king what he had seen. The king had decided that stealing food from Ife would be easier than trying to grow it. The hunter had warned him, though, that Ife had many warriors. So the king had dressed his men like egunguns. He had guessed that the people of Ife would be too scared of the spirits to fight back.

After many days the thieves returned to Ile-Igbo. They gave Moremi to their king. The Oba liked her. He made her one of his many wives. But he always watched her carefully. She could not run away.

Moremi now knew the true story behind the "evil spirits." But how would that help Ife if she could not get back to the city?

Before you read on . . .

> Pretend you are Moremi. Write down a plan for getting out of Ile-Igbo. Then write another plan for a way to fight the "evil spirits."

The Oba of Ile-Igbo guarded his new wife carefully. But Moremi was too smart for him. One night she got the king to drink a lot of palm wine. She gave plenty to the guards, too. Soon everyone was drunk and snoring. Moremi was sure they would stay asleep for many hours.

Moremi crept out of the king's house. She bought some ragged clothes from a beggar woman and put them on. Now no one who saw her could tell who she was.

Moremi hurried into the rain forest. She set out for Ife. She had to walk for many days. Each night she climbed a tree. She slept there, safe from the forest animals.

At last Moremi reached Ife. The people of the city were amazed and delighted to see her. They had been sure she was dead.

Moremi went straight to the king of Ife. She told him all about the "spirit" thieves. "They are only men," she said. "They wear masks and straw costumes to fool us. But we can drive them away so they will never come back." She told the king a plan she had thought of while she was a prisoner in Ile-Igbo.

The king of Ile-Igbo did not worry much when Moremi escaped. He knew how far it was to Ife. He was sure that Moremi would die in the forest. He saw no reason to give up his city's easy way of getting food.

So when the crops were ripe, the "evil spirits" came again to Ife. But this time everything was different. The people of Ife did not run away. Instead, they lit torches from their cooking fires. They stuck the torches into the robbers' straw clothing.

The straw quickly caught fire. Such a screaming and howling the robbers made then! They really did sound like lost spirits. They tore the straw off their bodies. Some did not get rid of it fast enough. They burned to death. Others were blinded by smoke. They ran into the points of the Ife warriors' spears.

Only a few of the "spirits" escaped into the forest. They ran back to Ile-Igbo as fast as they could. They told the king what had happened. The king and his people agreed that they should never attack Ife again.

The city of Ife, meanwhile, held a great festival. The people ate and drank, drummed and danced all night. Moremi, of course, was the guest of honor. The king himself thanked her. He gave her rich gifts. Everyone bowed before Moremi, the woman who had saved Ife.

Make Your Own Adventure

Suppose you learned that a gang of robbers was at work in your neighborhood. What would you do? With a partner, work out your ideas for protecting the neighborhood. Then share your ideas with the rest of the class.

Adventuring in Real Life

Follow your teacher's directions for these activities.

—— Reliving the Adventure ——

1. When and where did this story take place?

   _____

   _____

2. What was turning the rich city of Ife into a poor city?

   _____

   _____

3. Why did the people of Ife run away when the robbers came?

   _____

   _____

4. What did Moremi want to do first to fight the robbers? Why didn't the king want to let her do it?

   _____

   _____

5. What happened when the robbers found Moremi?

   _____

   _____

6. Who were the robbers? How had they found out about Ife?

   _____

   _____

7. How did Moremi get away from Ile-Igbo?

   _____

   _____

8. How did the people of Ife fight the robbers after Moremi came back?

_____

_____

—— Thinking About It ——

1. When did the robbers come to Ife? Why did they come then?

2. What clues showed that the robbers were really human beings?

—— Exploring Further ——

1. The story about Moremi is a legend of the Yoruba people. It is a tale of long ago that may or may not have really happened. (There is no reason why it couldn't have happened.) Read other African legends and folk tales in books in the library. Then choose an African story you like. With a group of your classmates, act out the story for the rest of the class.

2. With a group of your classmates, act out the story of Moremi in dance and pantomime. In pantomime, no one speaks. The whole story is told with gestures. You can use scenery, costumes, and props if you want to, but you don't have to. Try acting out the story for parents or another class that does not know the story. Can they tell what is happening?

3. Design a mask and costume for someone dressing up as a good or evil spirit. You might want to choose a spirit being you read about in an African story. If you prefer, you can use one from another people, such an American Indian people. Or you can just imagine one. Draw a color picture of your costume. Draw another one of your mask. If you can get the materials, make the costume, the mask, or both.

4. Learn about a modern African country. You might want to choose Gabon, where Mary Kingsley met the leopard. You might want to find out about Nigeria, where the Yoruba people live. Or you might want to choose some other country. Find out what tribes or peoples live in the country and how they get along. What kind of government does the country have? How do most of the people in the country make a living? What problems does the country have? How is it trying to solve them?

Adventuring on Paper

—— Exploring Words ——

In the story about Moremi you learned two Yoruba words, *oba* (king) and *egungun* (evil spirit). Neither of these words is usually used in English. English has borrowed words from many other languages, however. The words listed below are just a few of them. Look up each word in a large dictionary. Then write down what language or languages the word came from. Write down the word's meaning in the other language, too.

1. *dandelion*

   Language: _____

   Meaning: _____

2. *sherry*

   Language: _____

   Meaning: _____

3. *almanac*

   Language: _____

   Meaning: _____

4. *curry*

   Language: _____

   Meaning: _____

5. *port*

   Language: _____

   Meaning: _____

—— Exploring Sentences ——

One thing often makes another thing happen. The first event is called a cause. The second event is called an effect. For example, the robbers' stealing food made the people of Ife have nothing to eat. The food being stolen was the cause of the people's having nothing to eat. The people having nothing to eat was the effect of the robbers stealing food. Below are some causes and effects from the story about Moremi. Write a sentence to fill in the missing half of each pair of events.

1. Cause: The robbers looked like evil spirits.

   Effect: _____

2. Cause: _____

   Effect: The robbers found Moremi and took her to Ile-Igbo.

3. Cause: The "spirits" took off their masks and began to talk and laugh.

   Effect: _____

4. Cause: _____

   Effect: The king of Ile-Igbo decided to send people to steal food from Ife.

5. Cause: Moremi gave the king and guards of Ile-Igbo a lot of palm wine.

   Effect: _____

6. Cause: _____

   Effect: Some of the robbers were burned, and the rest ran away.

—— Exploring Further ——

Write a legend. If you want to, you can retell in your own words a legend or folk tale you have read. Or you can make up a legend of your own. Your story might tell about spirit beings. It might tell about animals that act like people. Or it might tell about human beings who lived long ago.

Tell or read your story to your classmates when you have finished. Draw a picture to go with the story if you want to.

Fire Wasn't Part of the Show

"In the moonlight, in the moonlight, in the pale moonlight," the sixteen young men and women sang. Their bodies swayed together on the theater stage. A soft blue light shone on them from high above.

The audience clapped and sighed in wonder. About 2,000 people filled Chicago's Iroquois Theater that Wednesday afternoon. Many were children. They were there with their mothers or nurses. On that chilly December 30, 1903, they were clearly enjoying their holiday treat. Certainly everyone felt safe. The beautiful new theater's printed program announced that the theater was absolutely fireproof.

The show was a musical comedy called *Mr. Bluebeard.* Its star was a comic actor named Eddie Foy. As the chorus sang about the moonlight, Foy was in his dressing room. He was getting ready for the show's next act.

Neither Foy nor the happy children saw what was happening backstage. The "pale moonlight" came from a floodlight above the stage. The light sat on a platform near the top of the stage's scenery. Soon after the song began, the floodlight started to give off sparks. The sparks made some of the thin muslin borders of the scenery catch fire.

Two stagehands saw the fire. They climbed to the platform. One tried to put out the tiny flame with his hands. The other tried to beat it out with a stick. The stick knocked bits of burning material into other parts of the scenery.

"Put it out! Put it out!" yelled William McMullen, the assistant electrician.

Another stagehand climbed up with a fire extinguisher. The extinguisher was a new kind. It was filled with powder. When it was sprayed on the fire, it did nothing.

By now the fire was creeping through the hanging material above the singers' heads. The singers saw it, but they bravely kept on performing.

35

A few people in the audience saw the fire, too. Most thought it was part of the show. "Look, a fire!" one little boy shouted. But he was quickly hushed.

Backstage, though, the noise was growing. More and more stage-hands were shouting, "Can't you see you're on fire up there? Put it out!" But no one on the platform was able to put out the fire.

Eddie Foy heard the shouting from his dressing room. Only half dressed, he ran backstage. His six-year-old son, Bryan, was watching the show from there. Foy thought perhaps a fight had broken out. He was afraid Bryan might be hurt.

Foy quickly saw what the problem was. By now the singers were near panic. One of them fainted. The audience, too, was beginning to be all too aware that the spreading fire wasn't part of the show. People started to stand up and push toward the theater's exits. A few children screamed.

Foy knew he had to act fast. The fire was a danger, but panic was a greater one. If people left the theater quietly, they would probably be all right. If they shoved and fought each other, though, many might be trampled to death.

Eddie Foy grabbed Bryan and pushed him toward a stagehand. "Get him out of here," he ordered.

Foy had taken off his costume. He was wearing only his tights. Half his face was covered with makeup for his part as a comic elephant. He looked very strange. But Eddie Foy didn't care what he looked like. As the curtain of fire danced over his head, he marched onto the stage.

Before you read on . . .

Pretend you are Eddie Foy. How can you keep the people in the Iroquois Theater from panicking? Write down what you will say and do.

"Don't get excited! It's all right!" Eddie Foy shouted to the frightened people in the Iroquois Theater. "Take it easy!"

The terrified singers by now had run off the stage. The conductor and some of the musicians, however, were still in the orchestra pit in front of the stage. "Play something—anything!" Foy shouted to the conductor.

Shakily the conductor and the musicians began to play the overture. This was the musical number that had started the show. As they played, the people in the best seats, on the floor of the theater, began to file out quietly. High in the gallery, though, things were not so quiet. In spite of Foy's words, the pushing and shoving had begun.

"Lower the fireproof curtain!" Foy shouted to the stagehands. They tried. But the curtain, which may not have been fireproof anyway, caught on the wires coming down from the floodlight. It stopped about five feet above the stage. "Cut the wire! Cut it, cut it!" Foy yelled. But no one seemed able to do so.

Performers, musicians, and stagehands began to run out through a backstage door. When the door opened, it let in a gust of wind. The wind blew a ball of fire under the curtain and into the front of the theater. Almost everything in the theater was made of material that burned easily. The flames spread everywhere in seconds.

Foy stayed on stage. "Go slow! Don't get frightened!" he yelled to the audience. He might as well have shouted into a hurricane. In the gallery, people were running and pushing like frightened cattle. Together they made a sound that Foy later described as "half-wail, half-roar."

Foy saw that there was nothing more he could do. The wig he wore was on fire. He wanted to make sure that Bryan had gotten out safely. So finally he, too, left the theater. With him went the last man who had stayed in the orchestra pit. He was a plump little violinist named Antonio Frosolono. Like Foy, Frosolono had risked his life trying to keep the audience calm.

Foy and Frosolono were not the only heroes of the Iroquois fire. A group of dancers were trapped in their dressing rooms high above the stage. An elevator boy named Robert Smith ran his elevator a dozen times to their level to rescue them. He dragged some of them out of their dressing rooms himself.

On Smith's last trip, the elevator itself was beginning to burn. Its control box was on fire. To hold the lever that would take the elevator down, Smith had to put his hand into the flames. He kept it there until the elevator reached the bottom.

Some audience members tried to help each other, too. Others cared about nothing except getting out. Women and children who fell were trampled ruthlessly by those behind them.

Worst of all, many people found that there was simply no way out of the burning theater. All but three of the building's thirty exits were locked. People managed to break down some of the doors. But later, when the fire was over, firefighters found most of them still closed. Bodies were piled in front of them.

The Iroquois fire killed 602 people. Hundreds more were hurt. Some were burned. Many others were trampled and smothered in the panic.

The bravery of Eddie Foy, Robert Smith, and others kept the numbers of dead and injured from being even higher. But everyone agreed that they were already much too high. After the Iroquois fire, many fire safety rules in Chicago were changed. People wanted to make sure that such a terrible tragedy would never happen again.

Make Your Own Adventure

Imagine you are the Mayor of Chicago. Make a list of the new fire regulations you would order after the Iroquois fire.

Adventuring in Real Life

Follow your teacher's directions for these activities.

—— Reliving the Adventure ——

1. Who were most of the people in the audience at the Iroquois Theater?

   _____

   _____

2. Why did they feel safe at the theater?

   _____

   _____

3. How did the backstage fire start?

   _____

   _____

4. What did the stagehands do to try to put the fire out?

   _____

   _____

5. What did Eddie Foy do after he got his son out of the theater? Why did he do it?

   _____

   _____

6. What did the musicians do to help?

   _____

   _____

7. How did Robert Smith save lives?

   _____

   _____

8. What killed the people in the Iroquois Theater?

   _____

   _____

—— Thinking About It ——

1. How would leaving the theater quietly and calmly have saved lives?

2. Some people thought the owners of the Iroquois Theater should have been charged as criminals. Do you agree? Why or why not?

—— Exploring Further ——

1. What plans does your school have for action in case of a fire? Ask your school principal or someone else who knows. What should people do if they spot a fire? What firefighting equipment is there in the school? What should students and teachers do if a fire alarm goes off in school? How does the school make sure that people there know what to do in a fire?

2. Next time you are in a theater or a movie house, notice the fire exits. How many are there? Where are they? Do you think all the people in the building could get out through the exits if there were a fire? If you can, ask the theater manager what plans the theater has for fighting fires. Ask what people in the theater should do if a fire breaks out.

3. Find out about scenery and lighting in theaters today. You might read library books about theater and stage design. You might talk to someone who works in a theater. What kinds of lights are used on stages today? How are they kept from starting fires? What materials are used for stage scenery? Which of these materials are fireproof or fire resistant?

Adventuring on Paper

—— Exploring Words ——

A compound word is made of two smaller words joined together. A number of compound words appeared in the story about the Iroquois Theater fire. They were made from the smaller words shown in the box below. Combine the words in the box to make as many words from the story as you can.

stage	back	light
flood	hand	fighters
proof	moon	fire

1. _____   4. _____

2. _____   5. _____

3. _____   6. _____

—— Exploring Sentences ——

Combine the short words in the box above with other words you know to make five compound words that are not in the story. For example, you might combine *light* with the word *star* to make *starlight*. Use each of your compound words in a sentence.

1. _____

2. _____

3. _____

4. _____

5. _____

—— Exploring Writing ——

An editorial is a piece of writing in a newspaper that expresses a strong opinion or feeling about an issue or event. It is usually written by the editor or owner of the newspaper.

Pretend you are the editor of a Chicago newspaper in 1903. Write an editorial about the Iroquois Theater fire. You might want to write about one of these things:

● Why Eddie Foy or Robert Smith should be given a medal for bravery

● Why the theater owners should be charged as criminals

● How and why fire safety laws should be changed

"Your Diamonds Were Bought with Blood"

"**I** am supposed to speak here tonight," Kate Barnard told the official in the small Oklahoma town. She named the public hall where her speech was to be given. "Is the hall ready for me?"

"Well . . . No, Miss Barnard."

"Why not? I reserved it in advance."

"Yes, I know. But, er, we found someone had scheduled it before you. It's full. Sorry."

"I see. Well, what about—" Barnard gave the name of another hall in town.

"Um, no, that's in use, too."

Barnard went through the names of every hall in town. The answer was always the same. The town would offer her no place to speak.

Kate Barnard knew that this was not just a mistake in arrangements. The town council had already warned her that they did not want her to speak there. Now, it seemed, they were making sure that she couldn't.

Or so they thought.

Barnard was a welcome speaker in most parts of Oklahoma. Women could not vote in national elections in 1907. In some states, however, they could run for office. That was what Barnard was doing. It made good sense. The office she was running for was one that she had created.

Oklahoma had become a state just the year before. Barnard had played an important part in shaping the laws that had become part of its constitution. Because of her, Oklahoma required all children to go to school. It had a law against child labor. And it was going to set up a Department of Charities and Corrections. This department would oversee programs that helped people. Barnard was now campaigning to be elected head of the department.

Barnard had persuaded farmers and workers to demand that the Democratic Party support the ideas she proposed. When the party agreed to do so, she worked to get Democrats elected to the Constitutional Convention. Largely because of her speeches, most of the men elected to write Oklahoma's constitution were Democrats. They had included her ideas in the constitution.

Barnard knew why the leaders of this town did not want her to speak here. Many of the people in the town worked for a nearby coal mine. A few months before, fifteen men had died in that mine. A fire had broken out there. The mine had only one entrance because the mine owner had not wanted to pay for two. When flames blocked that entrance, the miners inside had been trapped.

Barnard spoke against cruelty and unfair treatment whenever she saw them. The town leaders knew she would talk about the fire. She was sure to make the mine owner angry. He was a very powerful man, so they did not want that to happen. No wonder all the halls in town were suddenly full!

But if the leaders thought they could stop Kate Barnard, they were wrong. "Never mind the halls," she told the official. "I'll speak on a street corner if I have to. But I will speak."

And so she did. A large crowd gathered around Barnard on the street as she began to talk. But after she had spoken only a few minutes, a disturbance broke out in the crowd. Barnard saw a large, thick-necked man pushing his way toward her. He was well dressed, with a diamond stickpin in his shirt. His face, though, was that of a street bully. Clearly he was used to using force to get his way. Barnard had no trouble guessing that he was the owner of the burned mine.

The mine owner stopped in front of Barnard. Even though she stood on a low platform, he was taller than she was. Folding his powerful arms across his chest, he glared at her. He seemed to be daring her to go on.

Before you read on . . .

Imagine that this story is part of a play. Write a speech for Kate Barnard to make to the mine owner. In stage directions, show what Barnard does. If you want to, write a speech and stage directions for the mine owner, too.

The husky mine owner was a lot bigger than Kate Barnard. He was no braver, though. Kate glared back at the man with a look even more determined than his own.

Then Barnard set down the notes for the speech she had planned to give. Instead of going on with that speech, she spoke directly to the mine owner. The crowd seemed to hold its breath in order to hear her better.

Barnard pointed at the mine owner's glittering shirt front. "The diamonds you are wearing were bought with blood," she told him. "The blood belonged to fifteen men who burned to death in a mine you own. They died because you would not spend the money to build two entrances to the mine.

"You made their wives widows. You made their children orphans," Barnard went on. "You are responsible to Almighty God for the long, weary lives of poverty they face.

"I ask the people of this state of Oklahoma to elect me to the office I am seeking. If they do, I promise to change conditions like this. I will change them not only in your mine, but in all others as well."

For a moment there was silence. Then one or two brave people in the audience began to clap. Soon more and more were applauding. The mine owner could do nothing. Growling, he stomped away.

The people of Oklahoma gave Kate Barnard her wish. In the new state's first election, she was elected Director of the Department of Charities and Corrections. She got 6,000 more votes than any other Democrat running for office. By winning this post, Barnard became the first woman in the United States to be elected to a statewide office. She served for two terms. During that time and later, she did her best to make life better for all of Oklahoma's citizens.

Make Your Own Adventure

Look back at the story to find out what three laws Kate Barnard got into the Oklahoma constitution. Choose the one of these laws that means the most to you. Now pretend you are Barnard. Write a short speech that will persuade people to demand that this law be put into the constitution.

Adventuring in Real Life

Follow your teacher's directions for these activities.

—— Reliving the Adventure ——

1. Why was Kate Barnard making speeches in Oklahoma?

   _____

   _____

2. What three laws had Barnard gotten into the Oklahoma constitution?

   _____

   _____

3. How had she gotten those laws into the constitution?

   _____

   _____

4. Why didn't the leaders of the small Oklahoma town want Barnard to speak there?

   _____

   _____

5. How did they try to stop her?

   _____

   _____

6. How did Barnard reply to the leaders' action?

   _____

   _____

7. How did the mine owner try to stop Barnard from speaking?

   _____

   _____

8. What did Barnard tell the mine owner?

   _____

   _____

9. What happened to Barnard in Oklahoma's first election? Why was this unusual?

   _____

   _____

—— Thinking About It ——

1. What did Barnard mean when she said, "Your diamonds were bought with blood"?

2. The mine owner did not like Barnard, but in a way he helped her win the election. How did he help her?

—— Exploring Further ——

1. When did your state become a state? What were some of the laws put into its constitution? Ask a librarian or a social studies teacher to help you find out.

2. The Nineteenth Amendment to the United States Constitution gave women the right to vote nationwide. It was passed in 1920. Use library books to find out more about women's struggle to get the right to vote. Why did most men think that women should not vote? What did women do to change their minds? What women were important in the movement to gain the right to vote? Tell your classmates what you find out.

3. People involved in politics often make speeches. Like Barnard, they may be trying to win in an election. Or they may be trying to gain support for a change in some law or program. Find a political speech reported in a newspaper. (If you prefer, you could record one that is shown on television instead.) Then study the speech carefully. What does the person making the speech want people to do or think? What reasons does the speaker give for doing or thinking that thing? Do the reasons make good sense to you? Write down what you think the speech means and whether you agree with it.

4. How can citizens help a person be elected or help to get a new law passed? Work with a group of your classmates to make a list of ways. Then look in books about social studies or government. See if you can find any new ways to add to your list.

Adventuring on Paper
—— Exploring Words ——

A suffix is a word part added to the end of a word. The suffixes *-ment* and *-tion* turn a verb into a noun. Below are several nouns from the story about Kate Barnard. They have these suffixes. Next to each noun, write the verb that it came from. Use a dictionary for help if you need to.

1. arrangement   _____

2. constitution   _____

3. correction   _____

4. convention   _____

5. treatment   _____

6. election   _____

—— Exploring Sentences ——

Writers sometimes join two short sentences together to make a longer sentence. Doing this can make writing smoother and less choppy. Here are some words that are used to connect sentences.

and   but   for   or

Use one of these words to join each pair of short sentences below. To decide which word to use, you will need to think about the way that the meanings of the two sentences are related. Remember to put a comma at the end of the first sentence, before the joining word.

1. The town leaders thought they could keep Kate Barnard from speaking. They were wrong.

    _____

    _____

2. "I will speak in a public hall. I will speak on a street corner," Barnard said.

    _____

    _____

3. The miners had been trapped. The mine owner had not wanted to pay for a second entrance to the mine.

    _____

    _____

4. "You have made the miners' wives widows. You have made their children orphans," Barnard told the mine owner.

_____

_____

5. "I will win this election. I will make life better for the people of Oklahoma," Barnard promised.

_____

_____

—— Exploring Writing ——

Think of a law that you would like to see passed or changed. It can be a city, state, or national law. Then write a speech that will persuade people to agree with you. In the speech, tell people what change you want. Give reasons why you think that change would be a good one. Appeal to people's feelings, too, if you want to.

When you have finished your speech, let a partner read it. Ask your partner whether the speech has persuaded him or her to support the change you asked for.

Sybil Ludington's Midnight Ride

When she heard the horse's hooves, Sybil Ludington was putting her little brothers and sisters to bed. It was one of many jobs in the Ludington home that she had to do.

Sybil didn't mind the work. She was sixteen, and the oldest—almost grown up. She knew that her parents counted on her help. That help was especially important now, because her country was at war.

At least, Sybil hoped it was going to be a country. The American colonies had declared themselves free of Britain's rule the year before, in 1776. But the British king said that the colonists were just rebels. He said they needed to be punished. All over the colonies, red-coated British soldiers were trying to carry out that punishment. The colonists were fighting the soldiers for their freedom.

Sybil's father, Henry Ludington, was likely to be right in the middle of the fighting. He was a colonel in the colonial army. If fighting broke out here in Putnam County, New York, he would lead soldiers into battle. And the galloping hooves might be saying that that moment had come.

Sybil heard the horse stop in front of the Ludington home. She heard her father run out into the rainy evening to see who it was. Then the voice of a man Sybil didn't know began to speak to Colonel Ludington.

"I'm from Danbury," the man panted. Danbury was in Connecticut. That was the colony next to New York. "The British are burning the town. They'll come here next. Gather all the men you can and march at once. We've got to stop them!"

"I'll come with the men who live here," Colonel Ludington said. "But I don't know how we can call up those who live farther away. If I take the time to do it, we'll be too late to help you."

"I'd do it, but my horse is worn out," the man said. "Besides, I've never come to Putnam County before. I was told where you live, but I don't know about anyone else."

"I understand," Colonel Ludington answered. "But I don't know who else I can spare."

Sybil Ludington tucked the last of her sisters into bed. She kissed the little girl quickly. "Sleep well," she whispered. "I've got to go downstairs now. I have something very important to do for Father."

Before you read on . . .

> What feelings might have helped Sybil Ludington decide that she should do something to help her father? What do you think she is going to do?

Sybil Ludington ran downstairs. Her father and the man from Danbury were still talking outside. "I can call up the men in the countryside, Father," she said. "I know where they all live. And you know how well I can ride."

"But the storm might get worse," Colonel Ludington said. "And there are robbers and other dangerous people out there. Why, you might even run into the British before we do!"

"I'll never let them see me if I do," Sybil said. "And my stallion can outrun any robber! Let me go, Father."

Colonel Ludington finally agreed. He had no other choice if he hoped for a chance to save Danbury.

Sybil saddled her horse and rode off into the April night. She galloped through the rain past swamps and mist-covered ponds. Carmel . . . Mahopac . . . Mahopac Mines . . . Kent Cliffs . . . Farmers Mills . . . Sybil passed through them all. In each settlement, in front of every farmhouse, she shouted, "The British are burning Danbury. Gather at Ludington's!" Then, as soon as sleepy faces appeared in windows or doorways, she dashed on.

It was after midnight by the time Sybil came back home. She was soaked to the skin. She had ridden over forty miles in the past three hours. Both Sybil and her horse were very tired.

Sybil had done her work well. The yard in front of her house was full of men, guns, and horses. Her mother was pointing up the road.

She was giving the men directions for finding Colonel Ludington. Sybil found out that her father had left with the first group of volunteer soldiers hours before.

Exhausted, Sybil fell into bed. Only next morning did she learn the full results of her ride.

In spite of being able to leave right away, Colonel Ludington had been too late to save Danbury. The British had finished burning the town by the time Ludington and his men got there. Ludington caught up with the British, however, at another town called Ridgefield. By then, thanks to Sybil's ride, 600 men were with him.

At Ridgefield Ludington and his men joined a larger group of colonial soldiers. General Benedict Arnold commanded them. Together the soldiers made a surprise attack on the British troops.

The British soldiers were too tired to fight well. The colonial troops killed or wounded many of them. The rest quickly retreated to their ships in Long Island Sound. They never came back to Danbury or Putnam County. In time, the colonial army drove all the British soldiers out of America.

Sybil Ludington went back to her farm work. Later she married and had children of her own. She was proud that she had done her part to make sure that they could grow up in a free country. Her brave ride had helped the United States of America get its start.

Make Your Own Adventure

Learn more about the Revolutionary War. History books can help you. Find a battle or other event in the war that interests you. Imagine that you are present at that battle or event. How would you help the Americans? Talk over your ideas with a partner.

Adventuring in Real Life

Follow your teacher's directions for these activities.

—— Reliving the Adventure ——

1. What was Sybil Ludington doing when she heard the rider arrive?

   _____

   _____

2. Why were the American colonies fighting against the British?

   _____

   _____

3. What part did Sybil's father play in the colonial army?

   _____

   _____

4. What was the horseman's message? What did he want Sybil's father to do?

   _____

   _____

5. Why couldn't Sybil's father gather men from the countryside?

   _____

   _____

6. How did Sybil help her father?

   _____

   _____

7. How did Sybil know that she had done her work well?

   _____

   _____

8. What happened when Colonel Ludington and his men met the British?

   _____

   _____

—— Thinking About It ——

1. Why might the British and the American colonists have felt as they did about each other?

2. In what way was Sybil's ride a failure? In what way was it a success?

—— Exploring Further ——

1. In 1974 the United States Post Office put out an 8-cent stamp with Sybil Ludington's picture on it. What other famous people, besides presidents, have appeared on United States postage stamps? If anyone in class has a stamp collection, ask him or her to bring in stamps that show famous people. If no one has a stamp collection, look at pictures of stamps in a Scott stamp catalogue from the library. Choose a famous person on a United States stamp. Find out why that person was famous enough to appear on a stamp. Tell your classmates what you find out. Show the stamp or a picture of it if you can.

2. A man named Paul Revere had made a ride much like Sybil's a few years earlier. Revere's ride is much better known than Sybil's. This is partly because a famous poet called Henry Wadsworth Longfellow wrote a poem about it. Get a copy of Longfellow's poem, "The Midnight Ride of Paul Revere," from the library. With your classmates, take turns reading part of the poem aloud.

3. What songs did Americans sing during the Revolutionary War? "Yankee Doodle" is one song that you probably know. Try to find records, tapes, or sheet music of others. Play or sing them for your classmates. What do the songs show about the colonists' feelings at the time?

4. At the time of Sybil's ride, Benedict Arnold was an important American general. Look Arnold up in an encyclopedia or history book. How did he help the Americans? What happened to him later? Why? Write a paragraph or two telling what you find out.

Adventuring on Paper

—— Exploring Words ——

The story listed the names of some towns and settlements in Putnam County, New York, at the time of Sybil Ludington's ride. Below, list the names of five towns or cities near you (including the one you live in). Then try to find out what language each name comes from. Try to find out what the names mean, too. Chambers of commerce for the towns or a librarian might be able to help you. Write down what you find out.

1. Name: _____

   Language: _____

   Meaning: _____

2. Name: _____

   Language: _____

   Meaning: _____

3. Name: _____

   Language: _____

   Meaning: _____

4. Name: _____

   Language: _____

   Meaning: _____

5. Name: _____

   Language: _____

   Meaning: _____

—— Exploring Sentences ——

Two short sentences can be joined to make a longer sentence. Sometimes the meaning of one short sentence depends on the meaning of the other. When this happens, the sentence that depends on the other one begins with a word such as *when*, *because*, or *after*.

Join each pair of sentences below to make a longer sentence. Begin one of the short sentences with one of the words in the box. Choose the word with the meaning that makes the most sense. If you put this half of the longer sentence first, separate it from the other half with a comma. No comma is needed if you put this half at the end.

because	unless	when
before	after	

1. Sybil heard the horse's hooves.
   She was putting her little brothers and sisters to bed.

   _____

   _____

2. Her help was very important to her family now.
   Her country was at war.

   _____

   _____

3. The horse stopped in front of the Ludington home.
   A man began to speak to Sybil's father.

   _____

   _____

4. The men had to stop the British.
   The soldiers reached Putnam County.

   _____

   _____

5. Colonel Ludington could not get enough men.
   Sybil called up people from the countryside.

   _____

   _____

—— Exploring Writing ——

In **Make Your Own Adventure** you imagined yourself taking part in an event from the Revolutionary War. Now write about that event as though you were part of it. Use pronouns like *I* and *me* to show you were there. Tell what you did to help the Americans. If you want to, draw a picture of yourself taking part in the event. Put your story and picture up in the classroom so your classmates can see it.

"Don't Leave Me, Jim!"

"We need more horses," said General Ashley. "Moses Harris has said he will walk to the Pawnees to get some. Who will go with him?"

The twenty-nine men of the Rocky Mountain Fur Company were silent. No one was eager to go on that journey. For one thing, it was the beginning of winter. For another, the Pawnees lived three hundred miles away. That was a long way, even for men who were used to living outside.

Most important, no one wanted to go with "Black" Harris. True, the trappers respected the old mountain man. Everyone said Harris was a "man of great leg." That meant he could walk a long way without getting tired. He could live in the wild with very little food. He knew how to get along with the Indians. That was important for men like these who worked in the wilderness in the early 1800's. In those days the Indians still occupied most of North America.

But people also told dark tales about Harris. They said that once a man had been with Harris on a long walk like this one. The man had become too tired to go on. Harris had not tried to help him. Instead, he had left his companion on the trail to die.

Jim Beckwourth finally broke the silence. "I will go with Harris," he said. Beckwourth was one of Ashley's youngest men. He was eager to show Ashley that he could handle anything the older men could. He had another reason for wanting to prove himself, too. Beckwourth was sure he was as good as anyone. His father had been an officer in the Revolutionary War. His mother, though, had been a slave. Even here on the frontier, not everyone welcomed a man who was part African-American.

Before the two men left, Beckwourth spoke to Harris. "I have heard that if I give out on the road, you will try to leave me," Beckwourth said. "Please keep one thing in mind. If you do try, and I can still lift my gun, I will do my best to stop you."

Harris looked Beckwourth in the eye. "Very well, Jim," he said. "You may go in front of me the whole way. You can set your own pace. Then it will be your own fault if you tire out."

"That satisfies me," Beckwourth said.

Each of the two men loaded himself with twenty-five pounds of food and supplies. Each also brought a blanket, a rifle, and ammunition. That first day they walked thirty miles. At the end of the day it was Harris, not Beckwourth, who said he was tired.

Letting Harris rest, Beckwourth made up the campfire. He began to cook some of the food from the packs. Suddenly, though, he heard a shot from Harris's gun. A moment later a wild turkey fell out of a nearby tree.

Beckwourth loaded his own gun and soon shot a second fat turkey. He and Harris now had fresh meat for that night, and the next day, too.

The following day the men traveled forty miles. They made good time for the next ten days, too. On some days they were able to shoot birds or animals for food. On others, though, they had to eat food from their packs.

Beckwourth and Harris were very happy to see the Pawnee village at last. By then their packs were almost empty of food. They shouted to call out the Indians. But no one answered. The village was deserted!

"The Pawnees must have moved to their winter quarters already," Beckwourth said.

The two men looked for hidden food supplies that the Indians might have left behind. But they found nothing. They had no luck in hunting, either. The Indians of the village had long since killed most of the animals that lived nearby.

That night the wilderness seemed very big to the hungry mountain men.

Before you read on . . .

Harris and Beckwourth still have a long journey ahead of them. Which one do you think will get tired first? Why? What do you think will happen if one of the men can't go on?

Sitting in the empty Pawnee village, Moses Harris and Jim Beckwourth talked over what they should do next. "We had better head for the Nemahaw River," Harris finally decided. "We might meet some Indians there."

The men had to walk another nine days to reach the river. They walked far fewer miles each day than before. All they had left in their packs was coffee and sugar. They met no more fat turkeys in the woods, either. Both men were very hungry. Harris was almost exhausted as well.

Harris and Beckwourth did not find any Indians at the river. They did have one piece of luck, though. Beckwourth shot an elk. But they soon found out that the elk had been old and sick. Its meat tasted awful. Hungry as they were, they did not take any of it with them.

The two men went on walking beside the river. They moved very slowly now. They got rid of everything they could spare from their packs. They did not want to carry any extra weight. They even threw away their blankets.

After five more days the two came to a well-used Indian trail. They saw signs that Indians had passed along it only a short time before. The sight made Beckwourth feel better. Harris, though, seemed ready to give up. He lay down beside the trail. "This trail must lead to Ely's trading post," he said. "But that's thirty miles from here. I can't walk any farther."

Beckwourth tried to help Harris along. Harris, though, had meant what he said. He could stagger only a few steps before falling.

Now Beckwourth had a hard choice to make. "Harris, we will both die if I stay here with you," he said. "But if I leave you and go on ahead, I can reach Ely's in a day or so. I can get food and horses there. I will bring them back to you."

But Harris would not listen. "Oh, Jim, don't leave me here to die!" he begged. "For God's sake, stay with me!"

Beckwourth tried to help Harris along a while longer. But he felt himself growing weak from hunger. He knew that if he did not leave soon, neither man would make it to the trading post. Finally he decided to stop listening to Harris's pleas. He left the older man beside the trail.

Beckwourth was lucky. He had gone hardly half a mile when he met two Indians. Like Harris, Beckwourth knew how to speak the Indians' language. He was friends with most of the Indians he knew. In fact, because of his dark skin, many Indians thought that Beckwourth himself was an Indian.

The two Indians stared in wonder at the thin, staggering man before them. "You are dead! You are a ghost!" they exclaimed.

Beckwourth couldn't blame them. After so many days without food, no doubt he did look like a walking skeleton. He assured them, though, that he was alive, just barely. He also told them that he needed food and help for his companion on the trail.

The two Indians spoke to each other in their own language. Then one dashed away down the trail. He headed toward the trading post. The other went back with Beckwourth to the spot where Beckwourth had left Harris.

Harris heard their footsteps. "Oh, Jim! Come back! Don't leave me!" he moaned.

Beckwourth told him that help was on the way. Only a few hours later, in fact, several Indians on horseback galloped in from the trading post. They brought food with them. When Harris was strong enough, they put him on a horse. He was carried safely to the trading post.

Moses Harris was indeed a "man of great leg." But Jim Beckwourth, it seemed, was a man of even greater leg, and greater kindness.

Make Your Own Adventure

Suppose you are trapped in the wilderness. You have no food with you. How many ways to get food can you think of? How can you figure out which things you find will be safe to eat? Work with a group of your classmates. List as many ways for getting food in the wilderness as you can. Later, if this subject interests you, you might look in the library for books that tell which things are safe to eat.

Adventuring in Real Life

Follow your teacher's directions for these activities.

—— Reliving the Adventure ——

1. Where did General Ashley need men to go? Why?

   _____

   _____

2. What made Moses Harris a good companion for a long walking trip? What made him a bad one?

   _____

   _____

3. Why was Jim Beckwourth eager to go with Harris?

   _____

   _____

4. What agreement did Beckwourth and Harris make?

   _____

   _____

5. What did Beckwourth and Harris find when they reached the Pawnee village?

   _____

   _____

6. What did the two men do next? What problems did they have that they hadn't had before?

   _____

   _____

7. Why did Beckwourth leave Harris beside the trail?

   _____

   _____

8. What saved the two men's lives?

   _____

   _____

—— Thinking About It ——

1. How was what Beckwourth did like what Harris was supposed to have done? How was it different?

2. Do you think Beckwourth was right to leave Harris? Would you feel the same if Harris had died before Beckwourth could get help to him?

—— Exploring Further ——

1. Look back at the story. Find how many miles it was to the Pawnee village. Find how many miles Harris and Beckwourth traveled the first two days. How many miles did they have to go after that? How long did the journey take them? How many days in all did they walk before reaching Ely's trading post?

2. In the early 1800's, many men wore hats made out of beaver fur. This meant that the fur of beavers was valuable. Beavers lived in the streams of the North American wilderness. Other animals with valuable fur lived there, too. Companies of men like General Ashley's went out to hunt and trap these animals. Because they lived in the wilderness for months at a time, these men were often called "mountain men." Look in library books to find out more about mountain men. How did they dress? How did they capture animals? How did they get along with the Indians? Write down what you find out.

3. Find out about how American Indians lived in the early 1800's. Look in library books or an encyclopedia to learn what groups or tribes of Indians lived in different parts of North America. Choose a group that interests you. Then look for books or magazine articles that tell about its way of life. What did that group eat? What kind of clothes did they wear? What kind of homes did they live in? What stories did they tell? If you like, draw pictures that show the Indians' way of life.

4. Jim Beckwourth was only one of the many African-Americans who helped to settle the American West. Nat Love and Bill Pickett were two others. They were cowboys. Luticcia Butler was another. She was a nurse. Ask a librarian to help you find out about these or other African-Americans who lived in the West. Tell your classmates what you learn.

Adventuring on Paper
—— Exploring Words ——

Many names of places in the United States come from Indian words. Look at a map of your county. Can you find any place names in it that you think are Indian words? If you can't find any in your county, look for Indian names on a large map of your state.

Write down five Indian place names below. Write what kind of place each one names (a town, a river, a lake, or whatever). If you can find out, write what Indian language or group each name comes from and what the name means.

1. Name: _____

   Indian language: _____

   Kind of place: _____

   Meaning: _____

2. Name: _____

   Indian language: _____

   Kind of place: _____

   Meaning: _____

3. Name: _____

   Indian language: _____

   Kind of place: _____

   Meaning: _____

4. Name: _____

   Indian language: _____

   Kind of place: _____

   Meaning: _____

5. Name: _____

   Indian language: _____

   Kind of place: _____

   Meaning: _____

—— Exploring Sentences ——

Speakers and writers sometimes use unusual comparisons to describe people. For example, the mountain men said that someone who could walk a long way was a "man of great leg." Make up your own comparisons to describe each of the people below. Rewrite the sentences using your comparisons.

1. Mary is very kind.

   _____

2. Tyrone always gets into trouble.

   _____

3. Stephanie loves to argue.

   _____

4. Nguyen gets A's in every class.

   _____

5. Rachel thinks about nothing but pretty clothes.

   _____

—— Exploring Writing ——

Think about a time when you had a hard choice to make. Write a few sentences or paragraphs about what happened. (If you can't think of a time or you don't want to write about what happened to you, make up a story about someone who has to make a hard choice.) What choices could you have made? Why was it hard to choose? What choice did you finally make? What helped you decide? What happened because of the choice you made? Do you think your choice was a good one?

Chimpanzee Attack

Jane Goodall thought she would give anything to make contact with a wild chimpanzee. She had come to Africa to study the big apes. They were closely related to human beings. She wanted to know how they lived in the wild. But they ran away almost every time they saw her.

Goodall was working near a stream called Gombe. It was in the East African country of Tanzania. On this morning she was sitting on one side of a narrow ravine. A tree full of fruit stood on the other side. It was a kind of fruit that chimpanzees loved to eat. Goodall hoped that the apes would go to the tree before they saw her. Once they were busy eating, they might not run away.

Now Goodall heard leaves rustling behind her. She heard footsteps, too. The chimpanzees were coming! She lay down and held still. A plastic sheet covered her. It protected her from the rain.

Suddenly the footsteps stopped. "Hoo?" a voice said softly. Goodall knew that chimpanzees made that sound when they were worried or afraid. One of the animals must have seen her.

After a moment the footsteps came closer. Then they began to run. A terrible scream sounded almost in Goodall's ear.

Goodall looked up. A large male chimpanzee was climbing into a tree next to her. He moved through the branches until he was above her. He was only ten feet away. He screamed at her with short, sharp barks.

Goodall stared into the chimpanzee's dark face. She could see his brown eyes. She could also see his yellow, pointed teeth.

Most people know about chimpanzees only from movies or the zoo. They may think these animals are cute or funny. Goodall knew better. A grown male chimpanzee is much stronger than a human being. This one could hurt her badly or even kill her if he wanted to.

The chimpanzee shook a big branch. Twigs from it showered down on Goodall's plastic sheet. He hit the tree's trunk, too. Goodall knew that this was the way chimpanzees showed anger.

Then Goodall noticed something in another nearby tree. A female chimpanzee sat there. A tiny baby clung to her fur. A young chimpanzee sat next to her. They did not shake branches or scream. Instead, they watched her quietly with big eyes.

Suddenly the male's screaming stopped. He had backed away a little. Goodall could no longer see him. She knew he was still there, though. She could hear his breathing. What was he going to do now?

Goodall found out quickly enough. She heard one loud, barking yell. Then something hit the back of her head—hard.

Before you read on . . .

How is Jane Goodall's problem like Mary Kingsley's problem with the leopard? Do you think Goodall will do something like what Kingsley did?

All the time the male chimpanzee had screamed at her, Jane Goodall had held still. She had not wanted to make him even more angry. When he hit her, though, she decided she had to do something. She sat up slowly and turned around.

The chimpanzee stood there looking at her. He was still breathing fast. For a moment Goodall was afraid that he was going to charge at her. If he did, she might be badly hurt. She had heard about an African who was hit by an angry chimpanzee. The man had lost an eye and part of his cheek.

But then the chimpanzee moved away. After a moment the female chimpanzee and her babies climbed out of the other tree. They followed after the male.

All the chimpanzees looked back at Goodall often as they walked. The male hit some of the trees he passed. He seemed to be warning Goodall not to follow the group. He need not have worried. The shaken Goodall stayed where she was until the apes had disappeared into the forest.

Later she told a friend, an older man, about what had happened. His name was L.S.B. Leakey. He was a famous scientist. He and his wife,

Mary, had learned much about early humans. Leakey had lived and worked in Africa most of his life. He knew a lot about the animals that lived there, too.

"You did exactly the right thing," Leakey told Goodall. "If you had waved your arms or yelled, the chimpanzee would have thought you wanted to fight him. He might have killed you."

"I guess he just wanted to make me move so he could see what I was," Goodall said. "He never had seen anything like me and my plastic sheet before. He must have been as curious about me as I was about him."

Goodall thought a moment. "Well, I did get what I had been wishing for," she added. She laughed a little. "I certainly made contact with a wild chimpanzee. Or at least he made contact with me!"

Make Your Own Adventure

You don't have to go to Africa to watch and learn about animals. You can watch a cat or dog if you have one. Or you can watch birds or small animals in a park. Spend an afternoon watching one or more animals. Take a notebook with you. Write down everything the animal does. Write down how long it spends doing each thing. If the animal eats, what does it eat? If the animal meets other animals, what happens when they meet? Do they fight or chase each other? If so, who wins? Does the animal seem to enjoy being with other animals, or does it try to be alone?

Adventuring in Real Life

Follow your teacher's directions for these activities.

—— Reliving the Adventure ——

1. Why did Jane Goodall go to Africa?

_____

_____

2. What did the male chimpanzee do first when he saw Goodall?

_____

_____

3. What did he do next?

_____

_____

4. What did Goodall see in a nearby tree?

_____

_____

5. What did the male chimpanzee do after he stopped screaming?

_____

_____

6. What did Goodall do then?

_____

_____

7. How did the chimpanzees respond to what Goodall did?

_____

_____

8. What did L.S.B. Leakey tell Goodall about her actions?

_____

_____

—— Thinking About It ——

1. What might the nearby female and babies have had to do with the way the male chimpanzee acted?

2. Suppose Goodall had done what Mary Kingsley did when the leopard came near her. What do you think would have happened? Why?

—— Exploring Further ——

1. Find out more about Jane Goodall's study of chimpanzees. Books and magazines in the library can help you. What has she learned about the way these animals act? What things surprised her most? Find out what other people have learned about chimpanzees, too. Some people have taught chimpanzees to communicate with human language. How do the chimpanzees "talk"? What do they say?

2. Chimpanzees and many other African wild animals are in danger today. Find out several reasons why. Find out how some African countries, such as Kenya, are trying to protect their animals. Ask a librarian to help you. You might also write to groups that protect animals, such as the World Wildlife Fund. Tell your classmates what you find out. Talk over ways to protect wild animals while still meeting the needs of people who live near them.

3. Find out more about L.S.B. and Mary Leakey. Where in Africa did they work? What did they learn about early human beings and those beings' ancestors? Write down what you learn.

Adventuring on Paper

—— Exploring Words ——

List the names of six animals. You might start with *chimpanzee* and *leopard*. Then look up each animal name in a large dictionary. Find out what word or words each name came from. What did the word or words mean? What language did the name come from? Write down what you find out.

1. Animal name: _____

   Came from: _____

   Meaning: _____

2. Animal name: _____

   Came from: _____

   Meaning: _____

3. Animal name: _____

   Came from: _____

   Meaning: _____

4. Animal name: _____

   Came from: _____

   Meaning: _____

5. Animal name: _____

   Came from: _____

   Meaning: _____

6. Animal name: _____

   Came from: _____

   Meaning: _____

—— Exploring Sentences ——

Most verbs show past time by adding -*d* or -*ed*. A few do not. The underlined verbs in the sentences below show past time in unusual ways. In these sentences, the verbs show present time. Rewrite each sentence so that it shows past time. Look in the story for hints if you need to.

1. Jane Goodall <u>thinks</u> she would give anything to make contact with a wild chimpanzee.

   _____

2. They <u>run</u> away almost every time they <u>see</u> her.

   _____

3. A tree full of fruit <u>stands</u> on the other side of the ravine.

   _____

4. Now Goodall <u>hears</u> leaves rustling behind her.

   _____

5. She <u>lies</u> down and <u>holds</u> still.

   _____

6. "Hoo?" a voice <u>says</u> softly.

   _____

—— Exploring Writing ——

Remember the animal you watched in **Make Your Own Adventure**? Pretend that this is a strange animal that people know very little about. Pretend you are a scientist who has studied this animal carefully.

Write a report about the animal. Use the notes you made when you watched the animal. Watch the animal again and take more notes if you want to. In your report, tell what you saw the animal doing. Then tell what conclusions you can draw from watching the animal. Is this kind of animal friendly to other animals of its kind? Is it friendly to human beings? What does it spend most of its time doing? Was the particular animal you watched stronger or weaker than others of its kind? Why do you think so?

"I Can't Get Through!"

Deputy Sheriff Les Brown had never been in this part of San Diego before. He hadn't expected to be here now. He hadn't expected to be working today at all, in fact. But another San Diego police officer had gotten sick. Brown had been called in to take that officer's beat.

With luck, Brown thought as he started work, he would have time this morning to drive around the area. A quiet morning would give him a chance to get familiar with the new territory. He should have a quiet morning, shouldn't he? After all, this was supposed to have been his day off!

But luck wasn't with Brown, or with someone else, it seemed. Brown's police dispatch radio suddenly called his car number. "Child choking! Handle Code Three!" the dispatcher's excited voice barked. He gave an address several miles from where Brown was.

Code Three! That was saved for the worst emergencies. At once Brown turned on the flashing red lights on his police car. He hit the siren button, too. He knew that every second counted at a time like this.

Quickly Brown reviewed what he knew about this part of the city. Highway 101, a busy freeway, was nearby. This early in the morning it would be packed with people driving to work. Even with his lights and siren going, he would have a hard time getting through.

But there was also another freeway near here, Brown remembered now. It was only partly finished. Not many people used it yet. And he was pretty sure that an exit on it led right to the street he wanted!

Brown's car roared through side streets. Then he was on the new freeway. One exit flashed by. Another. The next one should be the one he was looking for.

There was no next exit! A sign named the right street. But the exit ramp had not been finished yet.

Brown's car screeched to a stop by the side of the freeway. He looked over the edge of the road. A rough, steep hillside stretched down from it for many yards. At the bottom of the hill was a wide, deep ditch.

A network of peaceful-looking streets lay on the other side of the ditch. On one of them, Brown knew, a child was dying. Very likely he could see the street from here. But he couldn't get there! He had no time to look for another road that went around the missing exit. There was no time to call for another police car, either. What was he going to do?

Suddenly a voice spoke to Brown. "What's the matter, officer? Can I help?" Amazingly, the voice came from high above Brown's head.

Brown looked up. A giant earthmoving machine had come up next to him on the hillside. The noise of the freeway must have masked its roar. The machine looked about two stories high. Its driver sat in a cab at the top. The driver was looking down at Brown with worry on his face.

Before you read on . . .

> How could the driver of the earthmover help Brown? Write your idea on a piece of paper. Fold the paper so that the writing is hidden. Then trade papers with a partner. After you have read the second half of the story, look at your partner's paper. Did your partner guess what would happen? Did you?

"A child is choking to death!" Deputy Les Brown told the driver of the earthmover. "I have to get down there, but there's no road. I can't get through! And I'll never make it in time if I have to go around." Brown tried to keep the anger and frustration out of his voice. He knew he wasn't succeeding.

"Follow me, officer," the driver said. "I'll *make* you a road!"

Like a dinosaur waking from a nap, the giant machine slowly started to move. It rumbled down the steep hill, scattering dirt as it went. It left a flat track behind it. Just as the driver had promised, the track was a sort of road. It was bumpy, but Brown could drive on it. He followed along on the new "exit ramp" that was being made just for him.

At last the earthmover reached the deep ditch at the bottom of the hill. There the driver swung the machine's two giant scoops into action. Over and over the scoops bit into the hillside. They dumped big mouthfuls of dirt into the ditch. Soon the part of the ditch in front of the earthmover was full. The machine continued its "road" across it.

Following the earthmover, Brown's police car finally rumbled up onto a city street. It was the same street that had seemed so far away only a few minutes before. Still, those had been long minutes. Would the child still be alive?

Brown didn't wait to thank the earthmover's driver. He raced his car down the last few streets to the address he had been given.

A weeping woman stood by the house's door. She was holding a baby. The baby had turned blue from lack of air. Brown grabbed the baby from her. He gave it the special "hug" that he had been taught to give choking people.

As Brown squeezed the baby's chest, something small flew out of its mouth. Brown saw the thing hit the floor. It was a button. Luckily, the holes in the button had let a little bit of air into the baby's lungs. That had kept the child alive until Brown arrived.

A moment later, a fire fighter dashed into the room. The dispatcher had called him, too. He gave the baby oxygen. The child's color turned from blue to red. After a moment the baby began to scream. Brown could see that it was going to be fine.

Brown was still on his new beat the next day. He happened to pass the spot on the new freeway where he had stood so helplessly the day before. Then he remembered that he had not thanked the man on the earthmover.

Brown stopped his car. He got out and looked down the hill. Sure enough, he saw the monster machine at work. The driver saw him, too. The man waved. Then he drove his earthmover toward Brown. When he reached the top of the hill, he turned the machine off and climbed down.

The driver ran toward Brown. Something more than running seemed to make him out of breath. "The baby . . . The baby . . ." he panted.

"The baby's fine," Brown said. "You helped save his life as much as I did. Man, that was teamwork!"

"I know," the man said. "But I know something else now that I didn't know then." His voice dropped almost to a whisper. "That baby we saved was my son!"

Make Your Own Adventure

Pretend you are a police dispatcher. Imagine an emergency that you would call a "Code Three." Write down a short description of your emergency. Trade descriptions with a partner.

Now imagine you are a police officer. The dispatcher has just called out the emergency described by your partner. What would you do? Write down a short account of how you would handle the emergency. Give the account to your partner.

Adventuring in Real Life

Follow your teacher's directions for these activities.

—— Reliving the Adventure ——

1. Why was Les Brown working in a part of the city he didn't know much about?

   _____

   _____

2. What emergency did the dispatcher call?

   _____

   _____

3. Why didn't Brown want to drive on Highway 101?

   _____

   _____

4. What problem did Brown have on the new freeway?

   _____

   _____

5. Who helped Brown solve his problem?

_____

_____

6. How did this person help Brown?

_____

_____

7. What did Brown do when he got to the woman's house? What happened as a result?

_____

_____

8. What surprise did Brown get when he went back to the freeway next day?

_____

_____

—— Thinking About It ——

1. What are two things a police officer does when a Code Three emergency is called?

2. Why didn't Brown stay to thank the earthmover driver?

—— Exploring Further ——

1. Find out about first aid. How can you give a "Heimlich hug" to a choking person? How can you help someone who is losing a lot of blood? How can you help someone who is not breathing? Books about first aid can tell you these things. You may even find some information about first aid in the front of your telephone book. With a partner, act out a demonstration of one kind of first aid.

2. Ask a police officer or a paramedic from the fire department to come to class. Have him or her explain how he or she helps people in different kinds of emergencies. Ask the police officer or paramedic to show or describe some of the equipment he or she uses.

3. What construction machines are at work in your town or city? Keep an eye out for them. If you see one, make drawings that show what it looks like and what it does. You might want to write a sentence or two of description at the bottom of your drawings. Post your drawings on a class bulletin board.

Adventuring on Paper

—— Exploring Words ——

A compound word is made of two other, shorter words. Below are some compound words from the story you just read. Draw a line between the two parts of each word. Then combine part of one word with part of another to make a new word. It can be a real English word, but it doesn't have to be. Then make up a serious or funny definition for your new word.

Example:
New word: *earthdoor*
Definition: a door leading into an underground tunnel

freeway	hillside	network
earthmover	doorway	teamwork

1. New word: _____

   Definition: _____

2. New word: _____

   Definition: _____

3. New word: _____

   Definition: _____

4. New word: _____

   Definition: _____

5. New word: _____

   Definition: _____

—— Exploring Sentences ——

Many adjectives can be changed to adverbs by adding *-ly* to the ends of the words. Rewrite each sentence below so that it contains an adverb ending in *-ly*.

1. In a sudden way the police car's radio began to speak.

   _____

   _____

2. Les Brown reviewed what he knew about this part of the city in a quick way.

   _____

   _____

3. Only part of the new freeway was finished.

_____

_____

4. The streets lay in a peaceful way in the morning sunlight.

_____

_____

5. The driver of the earthmover looked at Brown in a worried way.

_____

_____

—— Exploring Writing ——

A story is usually told from the point of view of one character. The writer tells the reader what that character sees and feels. The reader imagines that he or she is that character. The story you just read is told from the point of view of Deputy Les Brown.

Rewrite part or all of the story so that it is told from the point of view of the earthmover driver. What will the driver see differently? What thoughts and feelings will be different? If you want, you can write the story as if the driver were telling it. Use pronouns such as *I* and *me*. Or, if you would rather, use *he* and *him* as in the story about Brown.

The Oak Island Money Pit

Sixteen-year-old Dan McGinnis loved to go canoeing. Indeed, he almost seemed to have been born in the water.

Many people in Canada's small Nova Scotia province were like that. Nova Scotia is almost an island. Only a narrow neck of land ties it to the rest of Canada. This means that almost everyone in Nova Scotia grows up near the sea. Nova Scotians in Dan's time learned to swim and use boats almost as soon as they learned to walk.

Dan had grown up in the little town of Chester. Chester was on Nova Scotia's seaward coast. It was near Halifax, the province's capital. Chester stood on the eastern shore of an inlet called Mahone Bay. Like many Nova Scotia bays, Mahone Bay was dotted with hundreds of tiny islands.

Dan McGinnis liked to take his canoe out and explore these islands. He never knew what he might see there. Why, he might even find pirate treasure! Dan knew that French pirates used to sail from Le Have, a settlement forty miles down the coast. He had heard, too, that Mahone Bay's name came from the French word *mahonne*. A mahonne was a kind of fast sailing ship that pirates liked to use.

On that summer day in 1795, Dan paddled his canoe about four miles into Mahone Bay. That was almost all the way to the bay's western shore. He headed for a little island that he had never fully explored before. It was different from the other islands in the bay. It was almost covered with red oak trees. For this reason, people around Chester called it Oak Island.

Dan landed his canoe on the curved beach of a little cove. It was on the southeastern shore of the island. Right away he saw that something more than oak trees made the island different. A huge rock lay near the shore, half-covered by the water. A bolt with a heavy metal ring on it had been pounded into the rock. Most likely that meant that ships had landed here often. Their crews had tied them to the ring. Dan wondered why the ships had come.

What was more, Dan saw a half-hidden path leading away from the shore. It went up a hill toward the center of the island. He followed the path through the oak trees. At the top of the hill he came to a clearing. A few stumps stood around, as if trees had been cut down there.

One tree was left in the center of the clearing. It was a huge, twisted oak. It looked very old. Dan noticed that one limb of the oak had been sawed off. The branch was about sixteen feet off the ground. Still, Dan could see scars on it that must have been left by ropes. In fact, pieces of an ancient rope still hung down from the branch in one place.

Most interesting of all, the ground under the branch was not level with the rest of the hilltop. It had sunk into a shallow pit. Dan was sure he knew what that meant. Someone long ago had been digging there!

This find was too exciting for Dan to keep to himself. He ran down from the hill and pushed his canoe back into the water. He was in a hurry to tell his two best friends what he had found. He wanted the three of them to come back, with digging tools of their own!

Before you read on . . .

Dan's two friends were named John Smith and Tony Vaughan. Write a scene in which Dan tells them what he has found on Oak Island. Have Dan explain why he thinks his find is so exciting.

Dan McGinnis returned to Oak Island with his friends the very next day. One friend, John Smith, was twenty. Tony Vaughan, the other, was only thirteen. Both were as excited as Dan about what Dan had found.

The young men took picks and shovels out of their canoe. In spite of the weight of the heavy tools, they almost ran up the hill. They stopped in front of the big oak tree. All three stared at the sunken ground beneath the sawed-off branch.

"Someone has been digging here, all right," Tony Vaughan whispered.

"Yes," said John Smith. "But were they digging to find treasure? Or were they digging to bury treasure? That's what I want to know."

"Well, let's find out," Dan McGinnis said. He poked his shovel into the ground and began digging.

The other two pitched in. The three friends began to make interesting finds almost at once. When their hole was two feet deep, they came to a layer of flagstones. "Those never came from this island," John Smith said. "The nearest they could have come from is Gold River. I've seen some like them there." Gold River was about two miles away.

"For sure they didn't walk here by themselves," Tony Vaughan pointed out. "I'll bet the pirates put them there to cover up their hole."

The boys used their picks to dig up the flagstones. Below the stones were more signs that people had been at work on the island. The boys found that they were digging in a round shaft or well. They could see the marks of picks on its clay walls. The shaft was about thirteen feet across.

By now night was beginning to fall. The three friends had to paddle home. They came back to Oak Island, though, as soon as they could. Day after day they went on digging. Slowly the hole under the big tree grew deeper and wider.

Ten feet down, the three came to a platform of oak logs. The logs stretched clear across the shaft. Their ends were buried in its clay walls. The outside of the logs were soft and rotten. "These have been in the ground a long time," Dan McGinnis said.

"I'll bet the treasure is right under them!" cried Tony Vaughan.

But it wasn't. The boys excitedly tore up the logs. They lifted them out of the hole. Beneath them were only more dirt and gravel.

The boys kept on digging. Twenty feet down they found another oak platform. At thirty feet there was still another. In between was nothing but dirt.

"This could go on forever," Dan McGinnis said. "The treasure must be huge. Otherwise the pirates never would have buried it so deep. But we can't get it out with just picks and shovels. We need something bigger."

"That takes money," John Smith pointed out.

"I know. And we haven't got any."

So the boys had to give up their treasure hunt on Oak Island, for the time being. It took nine years for them to get together enough money to start it again.

Dan McGinnis and John Smith both bought land on Oak Island. Smith, in fact, moved there. He lived on Oak Island until he died an old man in 1857. During all those years, the men dug whenever they could get money and machines. But they never found any treasure.

Since then, many people have dug on Oak Island. They have been just as sure as Dan McGinnis and his friends that a wonderful treasure is buried there. Some have formed companies. They have spent hundreds of thousands of dollars on digging machinery. They have found signs that some very elaborate underground work was done on the island. But they have not found treasure any more than Dan and John and Tony did. Do you think they ever will?

Make Your Own Adventure

Draw a diagram of the shaft on Oak Island. Put in all the things that the three boys found in their digging. Then make your diagram go deeper. Show what you think might be there.

Adventuring in Real Life

Follow your teacher's directions for these activities.

—— Reliving the Adventure ——

1. Why did Dan McGinnis think that pirates might have come to Mahone Bay?

_____

_____

2. What signs did Dan find that people had come to Oak Island long ago?

_____

_____

3. What did Dan think the signs under the big oak tree meant?

_____

_____

4. What did Dan do right after he made his finds on Oak Island?

_____

_____

5. What was the first thing the boys found after they started digging?

_____

_____

6. What was the second thing?

_____

_____

7. Why did the boys stop digging?

_____

_____

8. What has happened on Oak Island since then?

_____

_____

—— Thinking About It ——

1. Suppose the boys had found treasure. What do you think they should have done with it? Why?

2. Suppose you had some money and someone asked you to invest it in a company that was digging on Oak Island. Would you do that? Why or why not?

—— Exploring Further ——

1. Strange things have happened during later digs on Oak Island. The sea has flooded the digs several times. Four people were killed in an accident. An underwater video camera seemed to show a human hand buried in the shaft. Find out more about what has happened on Oak Island. Use the *Reader's Guide to Periodical Literature* to look for magazine articles about it. Use *Books in Print* to look for books about it. Ask a librarian or your teacher to show you how to use these references.

2. Look in the library for other true stories about lost or buried treasure. Choose a story that you like and tell it to your classmates. Where is the treasure supposed to be? What kind of a treasure is it? How did it become lost? What has happened when people have tried to search for it? You might want to make a treasure map to show during your talk.

3. Some people today hunt for treasure in their spare time. They use tools called metal detectors. Try to find out whether any store in your community sells or rents metal detectors. Look in the yellow pages of your phone book. A large sporting goods store might have them. If you find a store that has metal detectors, ask someone at the store to explain how to use one.

4. Find out about one of the provinces of Canada. Use history or geography books. What are the province's most important natural resources? Where are its biggest cities? About how many people live there? Write down what you find out. You might want to trace a map of the province, too.

Adventuring on Paper

—— Exploring Words ——

Each of the words below has something to do with the geography of a coastline. Look up the words in a dictionary. Then write definitions of the words. If you like, draw a little picture to help explain what each word means.

1. bay _____

2. cove _____

3. spit _____

4. isthmus _____

5. cape _____

—— Exploring Sentences ——

When you write a speaker's exact words, the words should go inside quotation marks (" "). If a sentence in quotation marks is followed by a phrase such as *he said*, the sentence should end with a comma instead of a period. When you write a conversation or dialogue between two or more speakers, start a new paragraph each time a new speaker starts talking.

Rewrite the conversation below to show the speakers' exact words. Use punctuation and paragraphs correctly in your dialogue.

Dan McGinnis said he thought pirate ships had come to Oak Island. He said he thought the pirates might have buried a treasure under a big oak tree. John Smith asked him how he could be so sure. Dan said he had seen a shallow pit under the tree. Ropes hung from the tree, too. Tony Vaughan cried that they should get picks and shovels and try to dig up the treasure themselves.

—— Exploring Writing ——

Suppose you found a buried treasure. You were sure that no one else would claim it. What would you do with the money?

Write a few sentences telling what you would do. If you like, you can write about the treasure and how you found it, too.